Photography Exposure

9 Secrets to Master the Art of Photography Exposure in 24 Hours or Less

James Carren

For more books by this author, please visit
www.photographybooks.us

Table of Contents

Introduction

Exposure is the key to your whole photograph, because your exposure, for all intents and purposes, is the photograph. Whether you're working in film or digital, exposure is the process by which you allow light onto the film, or into the lens to be digitally recorded, as the case may be. If you allow too little light in, then you have a picture that is underexposed. If you allow too much light in, then it's overexposed, and generally speaking, neither are good conditions to be in. Exposure can often be one of the hardest things for a new photographer to get a good grasp of, but it's extremely important that you do, especially if you are a film photographer, or would like to go that route eventually. I think a lot of people find it hard because it's the part of photography that requires you to do a little bit of math to get it right. People see numbers and fractions, and immediately become daunted. With a digital camera, it's too easy to just disregard learning about exposure, because you can look at it immediately and adjust up or down. However, if this is something that you do professionally, then you know it's best to know what you're doing, so you don't waste your client's time fiddling with knobs. And even though you can memorize exposure combinations for certain weather conditions if you want to, I find that it's much easier to just memorize your standard apertures and shutter speeds and go from there. Over time, you'll become able to go outside and make a reasonably educated guess as to what your exposure would be.

Throughout the course of this article, I will explain underexposure and overexposure, and how to avoid them. I will also explain aperture and shutter speed, how they work together, and what that ISO knob means. I'll explain depth of field, and how it's independently affected by both shutter speed and aperture. Then I'll move into the different shooting modes generally offered on digital cameras, and how and when to use them. I'll get a little advanced with the Zone System, equivalent exposure, and how to correct things both in Photoshop and in the darkroom if you make a mistake.

What is Exposure?

If you want to get really technical, exposure is defined as: the amount of light per unit of area that reaches your photographic surface, be it a piece of coated paper, a strip of film or an electronic sensor. All that really means is that it's the amount of light you're letting into the lens. If you think about it, photographs are made from light, which records the image onto the surface you choose.

As photographers, we control how much light is used to record the image based on several factors. For the camera, those factors are aperture, shutter speed, and ISO. Combined together, the values you enter into your camera tell it how much light you need every time. The trouble is, just as with computers, the camera is only as good as the information you input into it.

You decide your aperture, shutter speed, and ISO based on the conditions you're photographing in first, and on aesthetic preference second. If you have a dark scene, obviously, you need to let in more light to get a picture that is properly exposed, and vice versa.

So how do you tell if a photo is properly exposed? Typically, you want the subject of your scene to be well lit. When it isn't, this is called underexposure. Of course, this doesn't mean you aren't allowed to have shadows, but there is a difference between shadow and the image being too dark. You can tell if you have an underexposed image in several ways. For digital, the image will be too dark and important elements, particularly your subject, will not be clearly defined. You might also notice a lot of digital noise in your photos. This is especially prevalent when you're shooting at night or in low-lighted areas. If you're trying to see if your film is underexposed, then look at the density. If it looks all black or it's hard to make out the image, even on a light box, then your negative is underexposed. With underexposed photos, you lose detail in the shadows of your photo.

Overexposure happens when you've allowed too much light to reach the sensor or the film. This happens a lot on really sunny days, especially if you're shooting from about noon to two. Your brights and highlights will be way too bright, resulting in what is referred to as a blow out. In addition, if you shoot at this time of day, you'll also end up with really harsh, unflattering shadows. You'll know for sure if your highlights blew out by looking at your photo and seeing if there are any bright areas that should have had detail but don't. White garments, for example, lace, are really easy to overexpose and quickly lose detail. As for film, you can tell if it's overexposed if it looks too thin, or clear.

Whatever method of photography you use, it's always better to overexpose than to underexpose. When you overexpose, it means that at least the information got recorded and can probably be pulled out with some careful maneuvering in Photoshop. Whereas, if you underexpose, the information wasn't there to begin with, so you have nothing to pull from. In a later tip, I'll give you some pointers on how to fix up under and overexposed photos, because it happens, to everyone. But the main focus of this article is to teach you how to take a properly exposed photo, and to do that, I need to explain why the different elements of exposure work the way they do.

Aperture

Aperture is going to be the backbone of what you learn about exposure, and it's incredibly important to understand, though it can be daunting at first. Also commonly referred to as an f/stop, aperture simply means, how big the opening in your lens is. That is, how much light you're actually allowing into the camera in order to create the exposure.

Now, here's something that's going to sound scary at first, but it's actually going to make your life easier. F/stops get larger in number as the size of the opening in the lens diminishes. Seems counter intuitive right? Like it should be the other way around? You'd think so, until you learn that f stop numbers are based in fractions, and of course, 1/8 is bigger than 1/16, so f8 is a bigger aperture than f16.

My suggestion, to make your life easier, would be to memorize your f/stops. If you're working with a digital camera, you're probably looking at it, thinking something like, "There are so many numbers on this thing. How will I remember them all?" But if you're working with analog, (or if you have both) you know there are a lot less numbers on your camera. Why? Because most analog cameras only use standard f/stops, where digital cameras also list half stops. You can still stop down a half a stop on an analog camera too, it just isn't shown. Plus, I find that using half stops gets confusing for most people when they try to do their math to adjust for equivalent exposure (which I'll discuss later). So, in general, I'd stick to the standard f/stops, and go from there.

The standard f/stops are, from largest to smallest:

- F/ 1.4 (though a lot of cameras don't go up that far)
- F/2
- F/2.8
- F/4
- F/5.6
- F/8
- F/11
- F/16
- F/22
- F/32
- F/64

Now, don't get confused by the fact that I said a lot of cameras don't go *up* that far. The reason I say *up* is because, with f/1.4, you're letting in *more* light than you are with f/2, and so on. If you stop down, you're halving the light you just allowed into your lens. If you open up a stop, the amount of light doubles. So, f/16 is exactly half the light of f/11, and so on. There are some equations out there that can explain the math side of things, but I don't know about you—I was never the greatest at math, and I find that the equation tends to scare more people than it helps.

You should also know that aperture controls depth of field, which I will explain in another tip.

As you play around with f/stops and discover what sort of depth of field you prefer, you'll probably find that you have a preferred f/stop, around which you adjust your shutter speed. I typically find myself set on f/8 or f/11, because I like a fairly dreamlike image with some sharpness. Plus, f/11 is always a pretty good place to start on a sunny, nice day.

Shutter Speed

Shutter speed is the other essential half to the equation of exposure. Rather than controlling how much light is let into the lens, it controls how long that amount of light is let in for. And, while aperture controls depth of field, shutter speed controls motion blur. A slow shutter speed allows for more movement within a photo, while a fast shutter speed stops movement for a crisper, less dreamy, photo. As with aperture, there is also a list of standard shutter speeds.

They are:

- 30 seconds
- 15 seconds
- 8 seconds
- 4 seconds
- 2 seconds
- 1 second
- ½ second
- ¼
- 1/8
- 1/15
- 1/30
- 1/60
- 1/125

- 1/250

- 1/500

- 1/1000

- 1/2000

- 1/4000

There are more, these are just the most standard. As you can see, each shutter speed is a stop down from the last, halving the light that comes into the camera. You're going to adjust shutter speed and aperture in conjunction with ISO, which I'll talk about next. Different shutter speeds are good for different qualities of light, but remember you also have to select the correct aperture as well.

The longest exposures (ones a second or more in length) are going to be good for low light situations, such as night photography or a darkened room. The long exposure allows more information in these situations to be recorded, but it also means that you're allowing for more motion blur. If you aren't a big fan of that style, you should consider adding more light to your scene, or making use of a mounted flash. You can also crank up your ISO, but this produces more grain (or noise, if you're shooting digital).

Long exposures (a second or under in length) are good for capturing water movement or other slow movement.

Half a second to about 1/30 adds motion blur to a moving subject. I would also say that if you have an exceptionally steady hand, you can attempt to hand hold, with either analog or digital, at about 1/30. Experiment with this a bit though. If you're shaky like me, you may find that it's still best to use a tripod or speed your shutter up another couple stops.

One fiftieth to 1/100th is where I typically start for handheld photos. There will always be situations in which you need to hand hold, especially if you're in a high energy setting that requires a lot of movement such as a child's birthday party or a wedding ceremony.

1/250th to 1/500th is good for relatively fast action, and anything higher than that is typically used at things like sports events. These shutter speeds can also be good for capturing infants and pets crisply, since they don't hold still very long.

Later on in the book, I'm going to give you some examples of good exposure combinations for different weather and lighting conditions. I'm also going to explain equivalent exposures, which are combinations of aperture and shutter speed that allow the same amount of light into the camera (resulting in the same lightness or darkness of an image) while allowing you to change the amount of motion blur, or lack thereof, or the depth of field. Remember, changing shutter speed changes the amount of motion in an image. I would not suggest trying to change shutter speed to affect depth of field. Though some photographers think this works, I was not taught this way, so it just doesn't make sense to me.

When you're shooting, experiment with your shutter speeds and see which you like better. Remember though, unless you're shooting a conceptual project, most people do prefer pictures to be clear and sharp. If you're ever shooting and your photos appear a little "soft" (meaning fuzzy, not clearly defined) zoom in on them. If everything isn't sharp as a tack, you might want to make your shutter speed faster. That is, assuming that everything is in focus as it should be, which you should always check.

And remember, you cannot fix focus or shutter speed in Photoshop. If you are a seasoned photographer, you already know this, but if you're just starting out, it's possible you didn't. I can't count the number of times I've had clients come to me asking if I can make a photo sharper. The honest answer is, not really, no. Yes, I know there is a sharpen tool in Photoshop, but that really is for something like the tiniest bit of shake. The more you have to try to fix something with the sharpen tool, the more overworked and almost comic book like it looks. That's why it's important to have your shutter speed where you want it in the first place, and if you're not quite sure, shoot it again.

For all you analog photographers, you know that you can't see your image before you shoot it, but it is important that you examine your negatives with a loupe after the fact, because it doesn't matter how in focus you get the enlarger. If the negative is soft, it's just not going to work out. With both large format and 35mm, you should be able to see the individual grains of your image when you look through the loupe. If you can't, it isn't focused. If you focus it, and it still looks like that, then your image just isn't sharp.

Now, while we're on the subject of sharpness, keep in mind that a good photo doesn't necessarily have to be sharp everywhere, unless you just like to work in the style of good old f/64. (F/64 is both a very small stop and a photography group, who believed that everything should be sharp in a photo). In order for a photo to be considered in focus and sharp, you need to have at least one point of focus in the photo that is that. This is generally the subject, or sometimes a part of the subject, of the photo in question.

So, just a quick recap on everything so far before we move on to ISO.

- Shutter speed is the other half of the equation when it comes to exposure.

- Shutter speed is how long you allow the duration of an exposure to occur.

- A slow shutter speed allows for motion blur.

- A fast shutter speed stops motion.

- Photos are considered to be soft when they have motion blur or are out of focus.

- Zooming in or examining grain will tell you if your photo is sharp.

- Aperture is the size of the opening in your camera lens, and it tells you how much light is being let into the camera.

- Both aperture and shutter speed are fractions, and each is double the size of the smaller stop, or half the size of the larger one.

- Shutter speed is listed as fractions, so that should be pretty easily understandable.

- Whereas f/stops get smaller, the larger the number. For example, f/22 is a stop smaller than f/16, meaning it allows in less light.

ISO

Alright, aperture, shutter speed. Pretty simple when I break it down, right? So you're probably thinking, what do I need ISO for? ISO (or ASA, for those of you who are old school) takes us back to analog photography. ISO is a number assigned to film to tell you how sensitive to light it is. Different ISOs are good for different light situations, although I guess theoretically, you could use any ISO in any situation as long as you adjusted accordingly. Again, that's theoretically. I tend to like to start with an ISO 400 film (or set my ISO there), because it's smack in the middle of the spectrum, meaning it's pretty good for your average sunny day or the average well lit room.

Now, while I suggest you start out with 400 ISO, that doesn't mean you have to stay there. Low ISO films (such as 200 or 100) produce less noise, or grain, which gives you a much smoother image. It also means that it's less sensitive to light, which in turn means you have to expose longer. Higher ISOs, such as 800, 1600 and 3200, are faster, allowing more light in quicker. They're typically used in low light situations where you've decided you don't want that motion blur, but there's a trade off. In place of motion blur, you get grain, or noise, if you're digital. While grain isn't necessarily a bad thing (some people really like how it looks) too much of it can get overwhelming and distract from the overall quality of the image. Color grain is especially bad when there's a lot of it, and it's really hard to clean up, so if you don't like it, I'd suggest a lower ISO.

So, let's talk a little bit about film grain. This will hopefully help you to understand how grain affects your image, as well as the difference between how color and black and white grain work. I'll also explain the difference between pixels that make up digital imagery, and traditional film grain.

Let's start with the film, since it's where many of our photographic principles and understanding come from. We use the terminology from analog photography to understand digital, and I have found that most photographers, myself included, become much better at their craft after having had some experience with a darkroom.

While I am by no means an expert or a professor on the subject, here is my general understanding of how the process works. Film is made up of gelatin, on which there is a layer of emulsion. Emulsion is the surface upon which the image is created. In the emulsion are silver halide particles. Silver, as you may know, is the most common reactive substance used in photography, though there are others. When you expose the silver to light, the light records the image it sees onto the gelatin. Basically, the silver halide particles get all excited and jump around, and they create the grain of your image. Grain is what makes up the resolution, or quality, of your image. The higher the resolution the better (although in digital photography the typical image resolution tends to be about 300). Now, here's where things may get a little confusing. Typically, when we say that an image has high grain, we are saying that it has lower resolution. This is because there is much more space between the particles, which means that the particles have to be larger in order to fill that space. And when particles get larger, guess what? You can see them more easily. This is why excessive grain is usually considered to be distracting to an image, because you're more observant of the grain pattern than the image.

What's so different about color film, though? Well, it generally works in the same way, with silver halide reacting to light, except that you also have to contend with the dye used for the color. The reason color grain is much harder to clean up is because the grain is made not just from silver halide, but from those dyes, which can commingle and create color casts as well. Color films are also naturally lower resolution than black and white, meaning that the film grains are larger, which will result in more grain being visible anyway. My take, whether this is strictly scientific or not, is that because the grains are larger, and have color casts, they're harder to clean up.

Next up, we have pixels. These would be your digital equivalent to silver halide crystal grain. The pixel actually makes up your image, unlike silver halide crystals, which do not. They're the smallest part of a digital picture. Essentially, the pixels are assigned a spot in a grid, in which they are arranged. If you have an image in RGB mode, then those pixels are going to be comprised of red, green, and blue. Alternatively, if you have an image in CMYK mode, then the pixels will be cyan, magenta, yellow, and black. This is optimal for printing because these are the colors typically used in printer inks. Basically, it's all numerical data. And the more pixels you have, the better. Just like with film grain, the more "dots " (pixels or grains) you have making up the image, the more resolution you have because they are smaller and there's less space in between them. And just as with film, ISO is going to directly affect your resolution, so it's important that you choose the lowest ISO you can. As I said in the beginning, ISO 400 is generally a safe bet, at least as a starting point, and you can adjust up or down from there.

Depth of Field

The textbook definition of depth of field is a little bit confusing, but makes sense once you think about it. It is: the amount of distance between the nearest and farthest objects that are in an acceptable amount of focus in a photo. The farther the distance you can see, the more the depth of field. So an example of a photo with a lot of depth of field would be a landscape. Typically with landscapes, you want the viewer to feel like they can see for miles. With shallow depth of field, the subject will be in focus and appear very close, but everything behind it will be a blur. How blurred is dependent on the f/stop you choose to use.

So let's talk a little bit about how depth of field is achieved. As with exposure, there are three elements. They are: aperture, focal length, and distance from the lens. With whatever sort of depth of field you choose, shallow or deep, there will be a spot where the focus is most optimized on the object. As the photographer, it's your job to find it.

As you know, aperture affects the depth of field inversely from what you might think. This means that, the larger the aperture, the smaller the number, and the larger the aperture, the shallower the depth of field.

Focal length doesn't really have to do with the length of the lens, but with the distance from the center of the lens to the sensor (or mirror in analog photography). A 50mm lens is considered to be standard, while less than 50mm is wide angle, and more than 50mm is telephoto. So by this logic, when you zoom in and your lens looks longer, you're going to have shallower depth of field. When you zoom out (your lens gets shorter), your depth of field is much deeper. Lenses with longer focal lengths capture less of an image from side to side, but allow you to get closer. So sometimes, you have to choose whether you want to be able to zoom, or be able to capture more of a scene from side to side. Every photographer, I think, should have a selection of lenses for different situations.

Finally, you can also alter your depth of field by physically moving closer to or further away from your subject. You might be wondering why you *would* physically move closer or further, especially if you have a telephoto, but there are lots of reasons. For one thing, if you don't have a telephoto, you might need to move closer, or if you have an extremely wide-angle lens, you might need to step back to get everything you want in. Plus, physically moving also changes your vantage point to your subject. No matter whether you think you know the photo you want to make or not, it's always important to move around and take some shots just in case you need them later.

Whether you're adjusting your depth of field by moving or by changing the focal length of your lens, you should know that the closer your subject is to the lens, the shallower the depth of field, and vice versa.

Modes and When to Use Them

Aside from full auto mode, there are four modes to choose from on any standard digital camera, be it Nikon, Canon, or any other brand. They all give you some type of control over the exposure that you're making, with full manual being the most advanced, because you're self-selecting both aperture and shutter speed.

Let's start with Program, because it's the most like full auto, but does give you the flexibility to make some exposure decisions if you would like to. What happens is that the camera goes ahead and chooses what it thinks the most optimal combination for exposure would be, based on the conditions entering your sensor. So let's say the camera has chosen its combination, but you feel that you want the photo to have a shallower depth of field. The camera will allow you to pick from different combinations of aperture and shutter speed that will give you an equivalent exposure. This way you have the flexibility to play around with both motion and depth of field. I find that this mode is especially good for new photographers, because it does give some degree of independence while still making sure you get a proper exposure. I feel like this mode is also a good way to learn equivalent exposures, the knowledge of which will allow you to comfortably use manual mode.

Aperture Priority and Shutter Priority give you even more independence than program, but still does half of the work for you.

Aperture Priority is self-explanatory—it makes aperture the priority of the photo. Say for example that you know for a fact that you want to shoot at f/22, but you have no idea what your shutter speed would need to be in the current conditions. With Aperture

Priority, all you have to do is set your camera to f/22, and the camera decides the shutter speed for you. It's optimal for when you know around what you want your depth of field to be.

Shutter Priority works in the exact same way, except that you make the selection of shutter speed, and the camera selects the aperture. I find that this is most helpful in situations you know you'll need an extremely fast or slow shutter speed.

These modes are the most helpful to intermediate photographers, who have some knowledge of what different combinations of aperture and shutter speed do in different conditions. They're also great for advanced photographers who want a little bit of a break.

Finally, there's manual, which is pretty obvious. If you're shooting manually, you've got to have a pretty good grasp on what combinations of aperture and shutter speed work well together in what conditions. This can take some time to get really good at. I would suggest trying to memorize some of the basic ones, but given some time shooting, you'll be able to judge a situation fairly accurately.

Equivalent Exposures

An equivalent exposure is basically an alternative combination of shutter speed and aperture that produces the same exposure as another combination. You might be thinking, if an exposure is correct, what would be the point of changing that out for another exposure that's going to let in the exact same amount of light? The answer is that your aesthetic can change dependent on what combinations you choose to use. As we've discussed previously in this book, aperture is largely responsible for the depth of field you get, and shutter speed controls how much movement there is in a photo, or lack thereof.

So let's say that you get a reading of f/16 at 250th of a second for your normal exposure. That's just fine, and maybe you take a picture and decide, eh . . . I want the depth of field to be more shallow and dreamlike. So, that means that you need to open up your aperture. Remember that when you open your aperture, the number gets bigger. Let's just say you want to open it one stop for now. Then you would be at f/11 and 250th of a second. The problem is, that picture is now going to be one stop overexposed. To compensate, you have to make the shutter speed shorter, letting in the light for a shorter amount of time. Shutter speeds get shorter as the numbers go up, so you would adjust by setting your camera to f/11 at a 500th of a second. Your depth of field is shallower, but the exposure remains the same. As you get a stronger grasp on the concept, you will be able to adjust your settings in this way more than one stop in either direction. For me, learning equivalent exposures was difficult. Rather than trying to do the math each time, I memorized the most common shutter speeds and f/stops, and went from there when I needed to. It's also a good idea to use Program mode in order to learn equivalent exposures. Of course, if doing the math each time is what works for you, then go for it!

Correcting for Over and Underexposure

No matter how good of a photographer you are, I can guarantee you that there will always come a time when you have a photo you absolutely love that is either over or underexposed. If the problem is too severe, then the image may not be salvageable. But typically, if you're just a stop or two over or under, then you can easily fix it in Photoshop, whether it's digital or film.

Overexposure

Let's start with overexposure. As with anything in Photoshop, there are several ways to fix the problem. For this you can either: use your highlights slider, use the multiply blend mode, or use Camera RAW. Of all of these, Camera RAW is the best and will provide the most correction to the image. But you can only use Camera RAW if you shoot on RAW. If you are a beginner, it's very likely that your camera may be set to something else. It might be jpeg, or tiff. If it is, switch it now. Always shoot on RAW from now on. The most image data is captured this way, and the most image data can also be recovered this way if and when you do make a mistake.

For shadows and highlights, go to Image>Adjustments>Shadows/Highlights. If you've only got two sliders in your dialog box, check the box labeled Show More Options. If you're dealing with overexposure, you're probably going to be working with the highlights slider the most, and maybe midtone contrast, although you can also correct shadows if need be. When you use shadows/highlights, you unfortunately can't open it in an adjustment layer. You'll be applying the corrections right to the image itself, and typically, you want to try not to do this. This is called non-destructive editing. To non-destructively edit, you need to open an adjustment layer, so that you can later remove or alter it if you need to. You have two options of how to do this. If you want to stick with highlights/shadows, using an adjustment layer isn't possible, but you can create a copy layer of your image, label it shadows/highlights, or overexposure, or whatever helps you to keep organized. Then you work on that copy to preserve the original.

If you do want to use an actual adjustment layer, click the half circle down at the bottom. You have the option of a layer called Exposure. From there you can non-destructively edit and go back and change things when you need to. Yet another option is to use the levels adjustment layer—it's only dependent on which you prefer.

Another option is to use blend modes, which is accessed by the dropdown menu in the palette labeled normal. Again, for this you'll have to duplicate your photo layer to work on top of, then change the blend mode to multiply. Repeat as needed.

Underexposure

Just as with overexposure, you can use the same techniques to compensate for underexposure, except that you would be dealing with the shadows and darks as opposed to highlights and lights. Again, you need to make sure you're editing non-destructively.

There's also a blend mode you can use to adjust for underexposure, and that would be screen. Try it out!

Now, there are other reasons you might also want to darken or lighten an element in a photo. It could be aesthetic development, or it could be because only a certain part of the photo ended up too dark or too light. For things like this, you'll want to select the dodge and burn tools. Dodging and burning comes straight from darkroom photography, and it's where you selectively make a certain area lighter or darker while leaving the majority of the photo at what is the relative proper exposure.

To dodge, in traditional darkroom photography, you would hold a piece of cardboard or another object over the area you wanted to lighten for a portion of the duration of the proper exposure. You would determine this by first making test strips for the regular exposure, and then making test strips of different dodging times to figure out the proper one. To dodge in Photoshop, select the tool, then select the range you want to affect, either midtones, shadows, or highlights. Select how much exposure you want to reduce it by, pick a brush size, and brush where you need the dodge.

To burn in traditional darkroom photography, you would make your photo at its normal exposure and then add on however much time you think you need, via the same test strip method. You would then use the cardboard to cover the part of the image you don't want to darken, and allow the rest to darken. In Photoshop, the method is the same as for dodging.

The Zone System

The Zone System is a method developed by Ansel Adams that is designed to give you a proper exposure every time, when correctly used. The thing is, it can seem a bit complicated when you first try it, but once you get the hang of it, it's one of the most useful tools you can have.

First, you need to understand the concept of middle grey. Middle grey is the color that is exactly halfway between black and white. With any scene you photograph, your middle grey is going to change, because you have a slightly different range of color in every scene. Don't get confused—middle grey doesn't mean that you find an actual grey tone in your image. You just need to find that tone, whatever it is, that's closest to middle grey. Your camera does try to do a pretty good job, but it often overcompensates. When a scene has a lot of light, you'll end up with an underexposed photo due to the overcompensation, and vice versa. In order to avoid this, what you do is focus your camera in on whatever tone your middle grey is, and allow it to take its meter reading from that. Then you stop down one to compensate, and shoot the whole scene on that meter reading, which will result in a fairly accurate photo.

So what exactly is the Zone System? Well, Ansel Adams took all the tones that there could ever be in a photo and divided them into ten zones, with middle grey being zone V (5). Zone VIII is pure white, and zone II is pure black (or zone X and zone I, depending on which chart you use. What matters is that, the smaller the number, the darker. Each zone is one stop difference than the one on either side of it. What you're basically trying to do here is make sure that you trick your camera into rendering the scene correctly. In analog photography, it's general practice to stop down one stop from what your middle grey reading tells you. The same is true for digital photography. If you're ever unsure of your exposure, especially with film, (or if you're unsure of what you want aesthetically in digital), I would suggest trying something called bracketing. Bracketing is when you find your middle grey exposure and photograph it, then move one stop up and photograph the scene again. Then, you'll need to move one stop down from your original exposure and do it again. If you start with middle grey and move five stops in either direction, you will have made your own zone system chart to refer to. It's also good to use bracketing when you have a scene that requires one exposure for the highlights and a different exposure for the shadows. This way, you can get the correct exposure for both, and then combine the two in Photoshop later.

This is just a very, very brief overview of what the Zone System is and how you can make it work for you. I would suggest doing some further research online and practicing the techniques I've mentioned in order to gain a fuller understanding. Hopefully, it will also help you to understand your camera better as well. A visual representation will also help some learners to see what colors, tints and tones are divided into what zones.

Conclusion

In this book, I have tried to cover every aspect of exposure that I can think of. Exposure can be one of the most trying things to learn about photography, in spite of (or perhaps because of) it being absolutely integral to the process. Now that you have an understanding of what exposure is and the components it's made up of (aperture, shutter speed and ISO), I hope you'll better understand your camera and have a better grasp on how to use it.

Hopefully, for those of you who are more advanced photographers, the discussion of equivalent exposure, the zone system, and the way film works were interesting and piqued your interest to learn even more about your craft.

I hope you go and try some of the techniques I've mentioned here, and find them useful. Remember, no matter how good of a photographer you are, practice is never a bad thing.

Did you Like "Photography Exposure"?

Before you go, I'd like to say thank you so much for purchasing my book.

I know you could have picked from dozens of books on this subject, but you took a chance with mine, and I'm truly grateful for that.

So, once again, a big thanks for downloading this book and reading all the way to the end—I truly appreciate it.

Now I'd like to ask for a small favor if you don't mind:

Would you be so kind as to take a minute of your time and leave a review for this book on Amazon?

This feedback will help me continue to write the kind of books that help you get results. And if you loved it, then please feel free to let me know! :)

More Books by James Carren

Portrait Photography - 9 Tips Your Camera Manual Never Told You About Portrait Photography

Landscape Photography - 10 Essential Tips to Take Your Landscape Photography to The Next Level

Photography Lighting - Top 10 Must-Know Photography Lighting Facts to Shoot Like a Pro in Your Home Studio

Photography For Beginners - From Beginner To Expert Photographer In Less Than a Day!

Photography Business: 20 Things You Need to Know Before Starting a Successful Photography Business

Photoshop – Master The Basics: Top 12 Easy Photoshop Tips and Tricks for Beginners

Photoshop – Master The Basics 2: 9 Techniques to Take Your Photoshop Skills to The Next Level